Guidelines to Improve Airport Preparedness Against Chemical and Biological Terrorism

Issued by Sandia National Laboratories, operated for the United States Department of Energy by Sandia Corporation.

NOTICE: This report was prepared as an account of work sponsored by an agency of the United States Government. Neither the United States Government, nor any agency thereof, nor any of their employees, nor any of their contractors, subcontractors, or their employees, make any warranty, express or implied, or assume any legal liability or responsibility for the accuracy, completeness, or usefulness of any information, apparatus, product, or process disclosed, or represent that its use would not infringe privately owned rights. Reference herein to any specific commercial product, process, or service by trade name, trademark, manufacturer, or otherwise, does not necessarily constitute or imply its endorsement, recommendation, or favoring by the United States Government, any agency thereof, or any of their contractors or subcontractors. The views and opinions expressed herein do not necessarily state or reflect those of the United States Government, any agency thereof, or any of their contractors.

SAND2005-3237
LBNL-54973 (II)
Unlimited Release
Printed May 2005

Guidelines to Improve
Airport Preparedness Against
Chemical and Biological Terrorism
(Unlimited Release Version)

Donna M. Edwards[†]   Phillip N. Price[*]
Susanna P. Gordon[†]   Ashok Gadgil[*]

[†]Systems Studies Department, Dept. 8114, MS-9201
Sandia National Laboratories
Livermore, CA 94551-0969

[*]Indoor Environment Department
Lawrence Berkeley National Laboratory
Berkeley, CA 94720

ABSTRACT

This unlimited release document is an extraction from the original Official Use Only report, Sandia National Laboratories report number SAND2005-1045 and Lawrence Berkeley Lab report number 54973/Rev 2.1. The purpose of the original document is to aid airport planners in defending their facilities against chemical and biological (chem-bio) attack, given the technologies and capabilities available today. With this document, airport planners should gain an understanding of the important issues for chem-bio defense, and should be able to assess the preparedness of their airport, to determine whether to bring in consultant expertise, and to target the most effective upgrades for their facilities. The defenses outlined in this document are intended to accomplish two objectives: (1) to deter some high-consequence attacks through HVAC system physical security, and (2) to mitigate the consequences of an attack through passive protection and active response measures.

Intentionally Left Blank

HANDLING OFFICIAL USE ONLY INFORMATION

The original report is determined to be Department of Energy (DOE) Official Use Only information. Official Use Only (OUO) information is certain unclassified information that may be exempt from public release under the Freedom of Information Act (FOIA) and has the potential to damage governmental, commercial, or private interests if disseminated to persons who do not need to know the information to perform their jobs or other DOE authorized activities.

Anyone who needs the OUO information to perform his/her job or other DOE-authorized activity may have access to the document. Such access is granted by the person in possession of the document. The information in this document may be included or reproduced to support the development of airport-specific emergency response plans, assuming that these plans are kept as restricted-access information, and that appropriate credit is given to the authors.

The following handling guidelines are requirements for Federal employees and contractors; airports should attempt to follow these guidelines to the best of their ability. Reasonable precautions should be taken to preclude access to the information by those who don't need it for official activities. To store it, if after hours building security is provided, it may be stored in unlocked receptacles, such as file cabinets, desks, or bookcases. If such security is not provided, then it must be stored in locked receptacles. OUO documents may be reproduced to the minimum extent necessary, ensuring that all copies retain the Official Use Only markings. Such documents may be destroyed by using a strip cut shredder that produces strips no more than 1/4 inch wide or any other locally approved method of document destruction. When sending it by mail, place it in a sealed, opaque envelope and write "To Be Opened by Addressee Only" on the outside. When transmitting OUO information by fax or email, use encryption methods approved for unclassified controlled information (e.g., Entrust) whenever possible. If encryption is not available and mailing is not a feasible alternative, then regular fax or email may be used. To process OUO information on a computer, the system must prevent access by unauthorized persons (e.g., use of password or file access controls).

SCOPE OF THE GUIDELINES

The guidelines in this document are intended to be general – to apply to *most* airports in *most* circumstances. But individual circumstances may vary, and all possible situations cannot be anticipated. There are specific circumstances in which this general guidance is not optimal. Some but not all, of these circumstances are noted in the text. The guidelines are based on the authors' current state of knowledge. That state of knowledge will evolve with time, and with it the advice may change as well. The intention was to give guidelines and the supporting reasoning, based on the current state of knowledge, to aid airport decision-makers now in applying this knowledge to their specific situations.

ACKNOWLEDGEMENTS

The authors extend their thanks to the personnel at the San Francisco International Airport who provided important insights into existing airport systems and plans, and collaborated extensively on assessments and testing to explore issues and options relative to airport chem-bio defense. In particular, we thank Dale Dunham, Neal Doten, and Timothy Hatfield.

In addition to the direct experience of the authors with various facilities, creation of this guidance for reducing the vulnerability of airports to WMD terrorism has involved drawing together the experience of many experts, either through direct interaction with the authors over the past several years, or through previously published reports addressing facility protection issues and options. The authors would like to acknowledge those who have contributed to this report through their work on facility defense programs and through discussions of facility protection issues. In particular, we would like to thank:

From Sandia National Laboratories: Mark Snell, Richard Griffith, John Brockmann, Wayne Einfeld, Fred Gelbard, and Larry Brandt

From Lawrence Berkeley National Laboratory: Tracy Thatcher, Woody Delp, David Lorenzetti, and Richard Sextro

From Honeywell Laboratories: Tony Faltesek

From Argonne National Laboratory: Anthony Policastro, Bill Dunn, and David Brown.

In addition, we thank Anne Platt, Ron Dykhuizen, Nate Gleason, Bill Swansiger, Todd West, and Caren Wenner from Sandia National Laboratories, and Tracy Thatcher and Woody Delp from Lawrence Berkeley National Laboratory for providing input and feedback on draft versions of this document. Additional reviewers provided feedback on the first published version of this report, including:

From the Environmental Protection Agency: Dorothy Canter, Les Sparks, Blair Martin, and Philip Campagna

From the Infrastructure Security Partership: Ralph Johnson

From the American Society of Heating, Refrigerating and Air-Conditioning Engineers, Inc.: Ronald Vallort

From the Department of Homeland Security: Charlton English

From the Metropolitan Washington Airports Authority: Tony Estrada

This work was funded by the Department of Homeland Security (DHS) Science and Technology Directorate through the PROACT (Protective and Responsive Options for Airport Counter-Terrorism) program.

CONTENTS

LIST OF FIGURES

\<Figures removed in the Unlimited Release version of the report.\>

ACRONYMS AND OTHER TERMINOLOGY

AHU	*Air-handling unit*
AOA	*Airfield Operating Area*
BW	*Biological Weapon* (or *Biological Warfare*)
Comm Center	*Communications Center*
C/B	*Chemical/Biological*
chem-bio	*Chemical and Biological*
CBW	*Chemical and Biological Weapon* (or *Chemical and Biological Warfare*)
CCTV	*closed circuit television*
CDC	*Centers for Disease Control and Prevention*
CW	*Chemical Weapon* (or *Chemical Warfare*)
DHS	*United States Department of Homeland Security*
DOE	*United States Department of Energy*
EOC	*Emergency Operations Center*
FOIA	*Freedom of Information Act*
HVAC	*Heating, Ventilating, and Cooling*
kilogram (kg)	*1000 grams or 2.2 pounds (a typical spray can holds approximately 300 g)*
LBNL	*Lawrence Berkeley National Laboratory*
LSZ	*Life Safety Zone*
micron	*0.001 millimeter or 0.00004 inches*
NIOSH	*National Institute for Occupational Safety and Health*
OUO	*Official Use Only (OUO) information*
PROACT	*Protective and Responsive Options for Airport Counter-Terrorism*
PROTECT	*Program for Response Options and Technology Enhancements for Chemical/Biological Terrorism*
SNL	*Sandia National Laboratories*
TSA	*Transportation Security Administration*
WMD	*Weapons of Mass Destruction (typically includes chemical, biological, radiological, and nuclear weapons)*

GUIDELINES TO IMPROVE AIRPORT PREPAREDNESS AGAINST CHEMICAL AND BIOLOGICAL TERRORISM

EXECUTIVE SUMMARY

The purpose of this document is to aid airport planners in defending their facilities against chemical and biological (chem-bio) attack, given the technologies and capabilities available today. With this document, airport planners should gain an understanding of the important issues for chem-bio defense, and should be able to assess the preparedness of their airport, to determine whether to bring in consultant expertise, and to target the most effective upgrades for their facilities. While airports, and particularly the *Transportation Security Administration* (TSA), have extensive experience with defense of aircraft against conventional weapons and explosives, there are significant differences for defense of the airport facilities against chem-bio attack. The intention of this document is to provide information and guidance with regard to chem-bio facility defense.

Planners should recognize that protecting a facility against chemical and biological terrorism will involve substantial effort beyond simply reading this document. Different groups will need to be involved: security personnel, HVAC engineers, maintenance crews, and all levels of airport management. Vulnerability assessment, attack prevention, and passive protection all require substantial planning and thought to identify what actions are or are not worthwhile. Several steps may be involved: identifying weaknesses, determining possible improvements and their costs, assessing the magnitude of the potential benefits, and choosing which (if any) improvements to make. The implementation of this report's "active response" recommendations will involve substantial pre-event planning, coordination, and training. Complex issues of communication, decision-making authority, and prioritization must be resolved in the pre-event planning since confusion in these areas can waste time, possibly with fatal consequences. These issues are beyond the scope of this document and must be resolved by each airport on an individual basis.

The defenses outlined in this document are intended to help planners accomplish two objectives: (1) to deter some high-consequence attacks through physical security of the heating, ventilating, and cooling (HVAC) system, and (2) to mitigate the consequences of an attack through passive protection and active response measures. The recommendations in this document are based on their ability to achieve these objectives. An evaluation of the cost of implementing each option is not included, since the expense will vary greatly for each facility depending on the current status of the systems in that facility. Instead, the effectiveness of various measures is discussed, and it is left to the individual facility to assess the cost of various measures and to selectively implement options that are both effective and affordable.

Detection systems are not included in this document for two reasons. (1) Both chemical and biological detection systems for building protection are in their infancy, and are not yet ready to be deployed as operational systems. This document is intended to help airports with the technologies and capabilities that are available *today*. (2) Detection technologies and protocols are evolving rapidly. A document that discusses detection technologies will need continual revision in order to keep up with the changes.

The guidance in this document comes from multiple sources. Sandia has gained experience in this area through several programs: collaboration with the San Francisco International Airport under the Department of Energy's (DOE) PROTECT[1,2] and PROACT[3] programs, which are now funded by the Department of Homeland Security; participation in the Department of Defense's Biological Defense Initiative[4]; participation in the development of the Centers for Disease Control and Prevention (CDC) / National Institute for Occupational Safety and Health (NIOSH) building protection guidance[5]; production of DOE's guides to defending DOE sites against chemical attacks[6,7]; and production of guidelines for the protection of U.S. Mint Facilities.[8,9,10] Lawrence Berkeley National Laboratory (LBNL) has long experience and expertise in airflow and contaminant transport modeling in buildings; LBNL contributed to the CDC/NIOSH building protection guidance and has produced a more recent guidance document for protecting buildings from a biological or chemical attack.[11] In addition to the experience of the authoring laboratories, the airport guidelines contained in this document draw from the U.S. Edgewood Chemical and Biological Center building protection document.[12] This airport guidance document is based on our state of knowledge at the time of publication. We expect to update this document as major new insights emerge.

The guidance is organized around discussion of the chem-bio threat, assessment of vulnerabilities, attack prevention through physical security of the HVAC system, and attack mitigation through both passive protection airflow control measures and active response plans. The starting point for facility protection is gaining an understanding of the threat: what is the history of chem-bio attacks, what are characteristics of chem-bio agents, what is the scope of the threat, and what are plausible release devices and plausible attack scenarios? Once the threat is understood, the next step is an assessment of the vulnerability of existing systems: what physical security measures, airflow characteristics, and response capabilities are already in place, and how do they deter and/or mitigate the consequences of an attack? Once the assessment is complete, the next step is facility hardening: what system upgrades and responses would better deter and/or mitigate the consequences of an attack? The facility hardening phase focuses on three elements: attack prevention through HVAC system physical security; attack mitigation by passive protection using airflow control, i.e., protection measures that will deter and/or mitigate the consequences of an attack even without knowledge of the attack; and attack mitigation through active response, i.e., actions to take in the event that a suspected attack is discovered.

The overview of the chem-bio threat describes the history and components of the threat to airport facilities, and culminates with a set of example credible scenarios. These different scenarios span the space of attacks that would be detected immediately (fast-acting chemicals such as sarin) to attacks that might not be detected for hours to days (delayed-acting chemicals such as mustard or biological agents such as anthrax spores). They include attacks in public areas, in areas past security screening, in restricted-access areas such as air-handlers, and in outdoor areas. <These sentences removed for this Unlimited Release version.>

Once the threat is understood, the next step for facility protection is an assessment of existing vulnerabilities and capabilities. The likelihood and/or severity of an attack can be affected by fixed physical characteristics such as HVAC physical security or HVAC characteristics, by technical capabilities such as the ability to manipulate HVAC systems remotely, and by personnel alertness, training, and coordination. Information from several airport departments is typically needed to successfully complete an assessment. The initial assessment should be an overview exercise, with the assessor gaining knowledge from consultations with subject matter experts, and perhaps brief tours of selected areas of the facility. For a more in depth assessment, the assessor should assemble a team of experts and possibly call in external consultants. A more in depth assessment might involve physical examination and/or testing of a representative set of systems, or of all relevant systems, depending on the extent desired.

The next paragraphs summarize the key points of facility hardening. Facility hardening includes attack prevention through HVAC system physical security, and attack mitigation through both passive protection (airflow hardening) and preparation for active response.

<These paragraphs removed for this Unlimited Release version.>

The purpose of active response is additional attack mitigation in the case of an identified attack. Response to a chem-bio incident includes response preparation and response procedures. The most important preparation for response to an attack is to establish and practice emergency procedures. This includes training of employees to recognize overt chem-bio events, and establishment and exercise of procedures to shelter people in place, evacuate people to quarantine, and decontaminate people. Additional important preparations include establishment and exercise of procedures to manipulate the HVAC system, to detain people at the airport, to locate unknowingly exposed people, to consider pre-screening of vehicles entering the pickup and drop-off areas, and to consider heightened security at curbside and at check-in.

The specific guidelines for response procedures depend on whether the attack is indoor or outdoor. The next paragraphs summarize the response procedures that are detailed in the report, with flowcharts included in the body of the report, in *Appendix D*, and as stand-alone heavy-weight cards.

<These paragraphs removed for this Unlimited Release version.>

This document shows the types of chem and/or bio attacks that an airport might experience. It shows a method for assessing a facility's hardness against such attacks and its preparedness for response, and shows the key steps that a facility might take for hardening and response preparation. This document gives guidelines for response based on the level of certainty about the attack. This document gives concrete steps that an airport can take to protect itself against chem-bio attacks. These steps are within the capabilities of systems and procedures that are in airports today. They do not rely on future technology revolutions or major expenditures. The systems and procedures already in place can be modified with modest investment to provide substantial improvements in an airport's defense against chem-bio terrorism.

1. Introduction

As potential targets of symbolic, human, psychological, and economic consequence, airports provide attractive terrorist targets. An attack with a chemical agent could cause mass casualties, a heightened sense of vulnerability, and worldwide economic disruption. An attack with a biological agent could contaminate and potentially close an airport for months, causing even greater economic damage. An attack with a contagious biological agent could cause a worldwide pandemic.

The purpose of this document is to aid airport planners in defending their facilities against chemical and biological (chem-bio) attack, given the technologies and capabilities available today. With this document, airport planners should gain an understanding of the important issues for chem-bio defense, and should be able to assess the preparedness of their airport, to determine whether to bring in consultant expertise, and to target the most effective upgrades for their facilities. While airports, and particularly the *Transportation Security Administration* (TSA), have extensive experience with defense of aircraft against conventional weapons and explosives, there are significant differences for defense of the airport facilities against chem-bio attack. The intention of this document is to provide information and guidance with regard to chem-bio facility defense.

Planners should recognize that protecting a facility against chemical and biological terrorism will involve substantial effort beyond simply reading this document. Different groups will need to be involved: security personnel, HVAC engineers, maintenance crews, and all levels of airport management. Vulnerability assessment, attack prevention, and passive protection all require substantial planning and thought to identify what actions are or are not worthwhile. Alternatives may need to be evaluated for cost and potential benefit.[*] Several steps may be involved: identifying weaknesses, determining possible improvements and their costs, assessing the magnitude of the potential benefits, and choosing which (if any) improvements to make. The conclusions must be re-examined if circumstances change; for example, actions that are not deemed cost-effective now might become attractive if there is ever a chem-bio attack in an airport. The implementation of this report's "active response" recommendations will involve substantial pre-event planning, coordination, and training. Complex issues of communication, decision-making authority, and prioritization must be resolved in the pre-event planning since confusion in these areas can waste time, possibly with fatal consequences. These issues are beyond the scope of this document and must be resolved by each airport on an individual basis.

The defenses outlined in this document are intended to accomplish two objectives: (1) to deter some high-consequence attacks through physical security of the heating, ventilating, and cooling (HVAC) system, and (2) to mitigate the consequences of an attack through passive protection and active response measures. The recommendations in this document are based on their ability to achieve these objectives. An evaluation of the cost of implementing each option is not included, since the expense will vary greatly for each

---

[*] Note that some changes will have benefits in more than one area; for instance, improvements to HVAC filters will improve preparedness against biological attack and will also improve indoor air quality in normal operations.

facility depending on the current status of the systems in that facility. Instead, the effectiveness of various measures is discussed, and it is left to the individual facility to assess the cost of various measures and to selectively implement options that are both effective and affordable. In addition, this document is not intended to provide advice to security screeners that would prevent the entry of chem-bio devices into security-screened areas, although any measures that can reasonably achieve this goal would be very worthwhile. Note that some of the chem-bio guidance recommended in this document may pertain also to radiological attacks, but that these were not considered explicitly.

Detection systems are not included in this document for two reasons. (1) Both chemical and biological detection systems for building protection are in their infancy, and are not yet ready to be deployed as operational systems. This document is intended to help airports with the technologies and capabilities that are available *today*. (2) Detection technologies and protocols are evolving rapidly. A document that discusses detection technologies will need continual revision in order to keep up with the changes.

The guidance in this document comes from multiple sources. Sandia has gained experience in this area through several programs: collaboration with the San Francisco International Airport under the PROTECT[1,2] and PROACT[3] programs, which were initiated by the Department of Energy (DOE) and continued under the Department of Homeland Security (DHS); participation in the Department of Defense's Biological Defense Initiative[4]; participation in the development of the Centers for Disease Control and Prevention (CDC) / National Institute for Occupational Safety and Health (NIOSH) building protection guidance[5]; production of DOE's guides to defending DOE sites against chemical attacks[6,7]; and production of guidelines for the protection of U.S. Mint Facilities.[8,9,10] Lawrence Berkeley National Laboratory (LBNL) has long experience and expertise in airflow and contaminant transport modeling in buildings; LBNL contributed to the CDC/NIOSH building protection guidance and has produced a more recent guidance document for protecting buildings from a biological or chemical attack.[11] In addition to the experience of the authoring laboratories, the airport guidelines contained in this document draw from the U.S. Edgewood Chemical and Biological Center building protection document.[12] This airport guidance document is based on our state of knowledge at the time of publication. Due to the diversity of types of WMD attack that may occur, the preparations and actions described here will not be optimal in all cases, but in the opinion of the authors the advice strikes an appropriate balance of all the objectives and issues related to chemical and biological defense. We expect to update this document as major new insights emerge.

The guidance is organized around discussion of the chem-bio threat, assessment of vulnerabilities, attack prevention through physical security of HVAC system, and attack mitigation through both passive protection airflow control measures and active response plans. The starting point for facility protection is gaining an understanding of the threat (*Section 2*): what is the history of chem-bio attacks, what are characteristics of chem-bio agents, what is the scope of the threat, and what are plausible release devices and plausible attack scenarios? Once the threat is understood, the next step is an assessment of the vulnerability of existing systems (*Section 3*): what physical security measures, airflow characteristics, and response capabilities are already in place, and how do they deter and/or mitigate the consequences of an attack? Once the assessment is complete, the next step is facility hardening: what system upgrades and responses would better deter and/or mitigate the consequences of an attack? The facility hardening phase focuses on three elements: attack prevention through HVAC system physical security (*Section 4*); attack mitigation through passive protection using airflow control (*Section 5*), i.e., protection measures that will deter and/or mitigate the consequences of an attack even without knowledge of the attack; and attack mitigation through active response (*Section 6*), i.e., actions to take in the event that a suspected attack is discovered.

Intentionally left blank.

2. Overview of the Chem-Bio Threat

The first step in facility protection is gaining an understanding of the threat. This section reviews selected historical chem-bio incidents (*Section 2.1*), discusses chem-bio agents (*Section 2.2*), discusses the scope of the threat addressed by these guidelines (*Section 2.3*), presents example release devices (*Section 2.4*) and example credible high-consequence scenarios (*Section 2.5*), and discusses facility-specific scenarios (*Section 2.6*).

2.1 Review of Selected Historical Chem-Bio Incidents

A brief review of some recent chem-bio incidents is presented here in order to provide a historical context for the recommendations in this report.

The infamous chemical attack on the Tokyo subway system by Aum Shinrikyo in March 1995 involved the evaporative release of sarin nerve gas in multiple trains converging on a single subway station. Packages leaking sarin were placed on five trains traveling on three major subway lines and scheduled to arrive at Kasumigaseki station within four minutes of each other at the height of morning rush hour. This station is located in Tokyo's government district, near the headquarters of many Ministries and in front of the National Police Agency. The attack killed twelve people, caused over 5500 casualties in sixteen stations, shut down two subway lines, and had a profound impact on the national psyche in Japan for some time afterward.[13,14] As such, the attack may have been successful from the point of view of the terrorist; however, a chemical weapon (CW) agent attack has the potential to be much more devastating. With a more efficient dispersal method, the impact of this attack could have been significantly larger, causing hundreds to thousands of fatalities.

Two months after the sarin attack, an attempt to release another chemical agent in the Tokyo subway was thwarted by quick-thinking subway guards. As hundreds of thousands of people were returning from vacation, a device consisting of two packages – a burning bag of sodium cyanide and a bag of sulphuric acid – was discovered in a restroom that (unlike most) ventilates to the passenger platform. The guards who discovered this so-called binary device doused the flames with water, preventing the fire from fully engulfing both bags and thereby producing deadly hydrogen cyanide gas. The four guards were briefly hospitalized, but there were no other casualties. However, if this device had gone undiscovered, it has been estimated that the resulting toxic cloud could have caused thousands of deaths.[13] At a minimum, it is likely that several hundred to a thousand deaths would have occurred.

Aum Shinrikyo did not confine its objectives to chemical attacks, but also attempted to release biological agents. The cult, whose membership included several trained scientists, used their vast financial resources to purchase large quantities of scientific equipment and supplies for producing bacteria and viruses – everything from culture media and air-filtration systems to electron microscopes and lasers. Although the full extent of Aum's activities may never be known, it is clear that they attempted to use biological agents at least ten times. In one instance, they used a sprayer and fan to release anthrax spores from atop an eight-story building in Tokyo. (Fortunately, the strain of anthrax used was relatively harmless.) They also may have used briefcases fitted with small tanks and battery-powered fans to spray botulinum toxin in crowded areas, including the Tokyo subway.[14]

The Rajneeshee religious cult likewise employed biological agents to cause harm to the public. In 1984, members of the cult contaminated food in the salad bars of several restaurants in an Oregon town called The Dalles with *Salmonella* bacteria, sickening 751 people, in order to impact the results of a local election. Cult members may have also used the attack as an "experiment" before attempting to poison the town's water supply. Seed cultures of the bacteria and the equipment needed to multiply them were obtained through mail-order scientific supply companies. A cult member who was a registered nurse supervised the production and dissemination of the bacteria. This incident illustrates the covert and ambiguous nature of bioterrorism, as it was considered a naturally occurring outbreak until cult members confessed. Before the recent anthrax mailings, this was the only biological attack in the United States known to have caused illness.[15]

In the well-known 2001 biological attacks, envelopes containing anthrax spores were mailed to prominent politicians and members of the press. It was fortunate in this case that the perpetrator(s) chose to disseminate the agent in such an ineffective manner, and to mail threatening letters along with the agent informing the victims that they had been exposed. This allowed the recipients and many others in their facilities to be treated before they became ill. Unfortunately, several bystanders were killed in these attacks because of unrecognized leakage of the agent out of the envelopes, particularly during mail sorting operations in postal facilities. The risk to those who had been in the vicinity of the contaminated envelopes en route through the mail system was not recognized until several fatalities had occurred. Two additional fatalities (one of them an elderly woman) with no obvious connection to the envelopes' source area, routes, or destinations also indicated the degree to which a very small amount of cross contamination may present a risk to the more sensitive portions of the population, such as the elderly and the immuno-compromised.[16,17]

In the past few years, increasingly there is evidence that terrorist groups are seeking to obtain and use chemical and biological agents. For example, in February 2002 disturbing evidence was found suggesting that a chemical attack on the American Embassy in Italy may have been planned. When a group of Moroccan terrorists was arrested in Rome, a large quantity of cyanide-containing pills (four kilograms of potassium ferrocyanide) was found in their possession. Such material can be used to generate cyanide gas. Ten kilograms of firecrackers, which contains enough explosive for a small bomb, and maps of the water network around the Embassy were also found in their possession. Soon thereafter, a breach in a utility tunnel near the Embassy was discovered.[18,19] To the knowledge of the authors, a connection between these discoveries has not been proven, but one can easily imagine a plan for a chemical attack on the Embassy that would explain them both.

Past use of chem-bio agents to cause harm to the public is not limited to these examples, but these provide a sense for the types of attacks that have been carried out or attempted.

2.2 Chemical and Biological Agents

In general, chemical and biological agents of concern for facility defense fall into four major categories:[*]

- **Fast-acting chemical agents** (e.g., sarin, hydrogen cyanide), which cause symptoms in seconds to minutes.

- **Delayed-acting chemical agents and biotoxins** (e.g., mustard, arsine, botulinum toxin, ricin), which are chemicals that cause no or few obvious initial symptoms and have action times ranging from hours to days.

- **Non-contagious biological agents** (e.g., anthrax, tularemia), which have no initial symptoms and typically cause flu-like symptoms after a few days or weeks.

- **Contagious biological agents** (e.g., smallpox, plague), which have no initial symptoms, typically cause flu-like symptoms after a few days or weeks, and are primarily contagious after the victims become symptomatic.

Among chemical warfare agents, in addition to the nerve agents that have become familiar to the public after the sarin release in Tokyo, there are also blister agents such as mustard, cyanide agents, pulmonary agents such as phosgene, and riot control agents. The many types of commercially available toxic industrial chemicals further broaden the chemical threat. Signs and symptoms can range from smelling a strange odor or experiencing nausea, breathing difficulty, or stinging of the eyes, to vomiting, seizures, faintness, or death. It is important to note that, in addition to the breadth of effects, the time to symptoms for chemicals and biotoxins can vary significantly from nearly instantaneous to several days depending on the agent. Therefore, there may be no visible casualties until well after an event. For example, nerve agents cause immediate symptoms and, with high exposure, can cause immediate collapse. However, a mustard-agent release in a populated area would cause no symptoms during the event, and may not become apparent until casualties begin to appear in area hospitals hours later. Other chemical agents cause some immediate symptoms but effects peak after several hours, so initial symptoms may not indicate the severity of the exposure. For example, phosgene can cause some initial symptoms followed by a symptom-free period before the most devastating effects occur, so this agent may initially be mistaken for a less harmful chemical.[20]

Biotoxins such as botulinum are toxic chemicals that are naturally produced by biological sources such as bacteria or plants. As chemicals that generally cause no symptoms for at least several hours, and possibly not for several days, these are grouped here with delayed-acting chemical agents. However, it is important to note that biotoxins are technically classified as biological agents.

Biological agent attacks can be even more difficult to recognize because these agents cause no symptoms for several days, and initial symptoms are typically flu-like. Unless the

---

[*] Further information on specific agents can be found on the Reference page of the Jane's website: http://chembio.janes.com/docs/jcbw/reference.shtml, specifically on the "Chemical Properties" and "Biological Properties" links.

biological agent is present in sufficient quantity to appear as a visible powder, as in the case of the recent anthrax mailings, it would most likely go unnoticed. For example, if such material were dispersed into the air, the resulting cloud of particles would most likely be invisible. Biological agents include, among others, *Bacillus anthracis*, *Yersinia pestis*, *variola* and *Francisella tularensis*, which cause the diseases anthrax, plague, smallpox, and tularemia respectively. In terms of responsive strategies, the main differentiating characteristic between these agents is whether or not the disease they cause is contagious. A non-contagious disease such as anthrax will only infect those who have been directly exposed to the spores. Contagious diseases such as smallpox, on the other hand, can be transmitted from person to person, and are therefore significantly more worrisome in terms of potential national and international impacts.[20]

2.3 Scope of the Threat Addressed by these Guidelines

In its entirety, the chem-bio threat represented by these agents encompasses more issues of concern than are addressed by these guidelines. Therefore, this document focuses on those threats with the largest potential consequences. The issues that are of primary concern include:

- Attacks with any of the chem-bio agents in each of the four major categories (fast- and delayed-acting chemical agents, as well as contagious and non-contagious biological agents)
- Airborne aerosol (i.e., liquid or solid particle) and gas releases
- Indoor attacks and outdoor airborne attacks directed at the airport
- Release devices including pressurized vessels, aerosolizers, and explosives
- Release locations including public areas inside the facility (both inside and outside security), as well as inside the air-handling system

Attacks such as these have the potential to impact large areas of the airport facility, causing injury or death to hundreds to thousands of occupants, and causing widespread contamination, including aircraft that were at the airport, the airport buildings themselves, and the surrounding areas downwind for several miles. Therefore, this document focuses on methods to prevent or mitigate releases of chemical or biological agents that can potentially impact an entire facility.

Additional threat areas that are important for the facility to consider but are outside the scope of this document include:

- Releases onboard aircraft
- Contagious person (biological)
- Food contamination (biological)

Releases onboard aircraft present an important concern, but are considered beyond the scope of facility protection, although airport response must coordinate with aircraft in the event of a chem-bio attack, whether the attack is located on the aircraft or in the airport itself. At a minimum, aircraft that may be contaminated should be physically separated from the facility if possible. Contagious people, particularly those who have been voluntarily infected and attempt to spread their disease intentionally, are a grave concern for biological agent attacks. However, this type of "vector" attack is primarily in the realm of the public health community, and is therefore not considered here. Food-borne biological contamination is also an important issue, but in itself would require an extensive analysis to determine the security of the food supply in order to prevent intentional contamination.

Finally, several types of attacks were were not considered in these guidelines because they would be relatively ineffective for the widespread dispersal of an agent at significant concentrations within the buildings. These include:
- Letters and packages
- Water contamination
- Injection (other than via explosive, e.g. by a needle)

Letters and packages are relatively ineffective devices for large-scale chem-bio attacks. Relatively few people would be injured by such an attack, unless a bomb was also in the package (and this situation is addressed in these guidelines). Significant contamination of water sources is difficult due to the large quantity of agent and the relative sophistication that would be needed. Chlorination and filtration further limit the ability of an adversary to effectively attack this way. Therefore, water contamination was not considered for these guidelines. Finally, injection of agent is typically only effective on the scale of assault on individuals (and has in the past been used in successful assassinations). Injection is not a credible method to injure large numbers of people, with the exception of explosive dispersal, where contaminated shrapnel can exacerbate the injuries caused by the explosion itself and harm first responders.

2.4 Example Release Devices

<This section removed for this Unlimited Release version.>

2.5 Example Credible Scenarios

<This section removed for this Unlimited Release version.>

2.6 Facility-Specific Scenarios

After reviewing the materials above, each facility is encouraged to develop a few threat scenarios more specific to their own issues and concerns. If they are viewed as sufficiently applicable, those scenarios listed above can be used. However, if the facility owner or local security professionals have certain concerns which are not reflected by these, additional scenarios should be devised to reflect these issues. For example, an international airport may be particularly concerned with threats associated with inbound international flights.

Such an initial set of scenarios can help provide food-for-thought during the assessment phase that follows.

As the assessment proceeds, these initial scenarios should be adjusted as appropriate. For example, if the facility owner initially feels that only attacks in the public area are credible, but this view changes during the site assessment, then attacks in the secure area should be included. Similarly, if attacks in the air handlers are initially a concern, but the assessment shows this scenario to be relatively unlikely, then this scenario can be dropped. When the assessment is complete, the final set of scenarios should include a handful of potential threats on which the facility plans to focus while considering options for facility hardening and response.

3. Vulnerability Assessment

Once the threat is understood, the next step for facility protection is an assessment of existing vulnerabilities and capabilities. The likelihood and/or severity of an attack can be affected by fixed physical characteristics such as HVAC physical security or HVAC characteristics, by technical capabilities such as the ability to manipulate HVAC systems remotely, and by personnel alertness, training, and coordination.

A lead department, such as the emergency planning department, should be chosen to be responsible for performing the initial assessment. Other departments must provide resources and expertise as needed. For example, *security* must provide expertise in HVAC system physical security systems, *mechanical maintenance* must provide expertise in HVAC operations, and *emergency response personnel* (including duty manager, communications, police, fire, and public health) must provide expertise in emergency response capabilities and preparation.

The initial assessment should be an overview exercise, with the assessor(s) gaining knowledge from consultations with subject matter experts, and perhaps brief tours of selected areas of the facility. The first step should be for the assessor(s) to read the rest of this document to see what types of information are needed. It might also be helpful to run through the Building Vulnerability Assessment and Mitigation Program (BVAMP), a computer program designed for general commercial buildings, and which is available in the "Vulnerability Assessment" section of the Lawrence Berkeley National Laboratory "secure buildings" website at http://securebuildings.lbl.gov. The BVAMP software is for generic buildings that are not specific to airports, so some advice may differ; where there is a difference, this airport-specific document supersedes the software.

For a more in depth assessment, the assessor(s) should assemble a team of experts from the above departments, perhaps including airlines and concessionaires as well, and possibly calling in external consultants in these areas. A more in depth assessment might involve physical examination and/or testing of a representative set of systems, or of all relevant systems, depending on the extent desired. As a starting point, the assessment team should use the "Report Card" in *Appendix A*, which highlights the key vulnerabilities of an airport to chem-bio attack.

The key vulnerabilities occur in three areas: physical security of the HVAC system, the airflow characteristics in the facility, and the response capabilities of the facility. The explanation of these vulnerabilities is described fully in the sections that discuss *Attack Prevention (Section 4)* and *Attack Mitigation (Sections 5 and 6)*. These explanations are not duplicated here; however, the following subsections highlight the systems that the assessment should examine. The key vulnerabilities that the assessment should address are listed under the relevant systems in the next three subsections: *Assessment of Ventilation (HVAC) System Physical Security Measures (Subsection 3.1)*; *Assessment of Airflow Characteristics (Subsection 3.2)*; and *Assessment of Response Capabilities (Subsection 3.3)*.

3.1 Assessment of Ventilation (HVAC) System Physical Security Measures

The extensive physical security measures in place in airports, primarily focused on keeping conventional explosives and weapons off of airplanes, will serve to deter many chem-bio attacks as well. However for the problem of protecting the airport itself, a primary concern is an attack in which agent is released directly into an HVAC system. For example, a release into a fresh-air intake, or into the return grilles of a system that recirculates a large fraction of the return air, would immediately contaminate the entire area served by that HVAC system (an area as large as several boarding gates on several floors, for example) due to the forced-air flow through the system, and then begin spreading into adjacent areas. Prevention of this category of high-consequence attack requires physical protection of the HVAC systems.

All components of the HVAC system must therefore be examined for vulnerability to terrorist access. These components include the building air intakes, the HVAC equipment and mechanical rooms, the HVAC control systems, the return air grilles, the HVAC exhausts, as well as general building information. Each of these components provides a mechanism for a high-consequence attack; these mechanisms are discussed in *Section 4, Attack Prevention*. The primary concern is *access* to these HVAC-system components. The assessment team should look for *any possible* route to access each of these components, and consider that *any* vulnerability could be exploited. The team must consider paths through public areas, paths through restricted-access areas, and means of defeating mechanisms for access prevention. The assessment team should examine possible routes of access to each of these components for each HVAC system, and recommend improvements as appropriate. Each of the components of ventilation system security are discussed in more detail and prioritized in Section 4, *Attack Prevention: Ventilation (HVAC) System Physical Security*.

3.2 Assessment of Airflow Characteristics

In addition to considering releases into the HVAC system, the assessment team must consider the airflow patterns in the facility and how these will affect the spread of a release. The pattern of air flows (and therefore agent transport) in a typical facility is largely determined by HVAC system operation. Vulnerability to chemical or biological attack therefore depends in part on HVAC system design and operation. The assessment team must examine how HVAC system design and operation affects airflow and agent transport by each of these mechanisms.

If an attack is detected rapidly and evacuation is initiated, the number of people exposed will depend directly on the rate of spread of the agent. If an attack is detected only after a long delay—as would be expected of many biological attacks—contamination is likely to be widespread no matter what the airflow conditions, and the number of people exposed will depend on many factors other than the rate of spread of the agent. But even in this case, a non-negligible reduction in casualties and contamination can be attained via improved airflow characteristics.

Assessment of the mechanisms of agent transport is discussed briefly in the following sections: Presence of airflows that can spread agent (*Section 3.2.1*); Air supply to critical emergency response functions (*Section 3.2.2*); HVAC filters, dampers, and fan operations (*Section 3.2.3*). Further direction on assessment techniques is provided in *Appendix B*, which gives guidance for the assessment of airflow among interconnected buildings (*Section B.1*) and for the assessment of airflow to critical emergency response functions (*Section B.2*). Each of the mechanisms of agent transport, and how to limit their impact, is discussed more fully in *Section 5, Attack Mitigation: Passive Protection through Airflow Control*.

3.2.1 Presence of airflows that can spread agent

HVAC systems may spread contamination rapidly over large distances, or they may contain it to the local area of the release. HVAC systems may spread agent from public areas to secure areas, or they may prevent the spread of agent from one area to another. HVAC systems operation may remove agent from the building and thus dilute the concentration of agent in the air supplied to the building occupants, or they may continue to circulate the agent within the building.

Ideally from the point of view of attack mitigation, if a chemical or biological agent is released, the resulting cloud of agent will not spread or will spread slowly. This will minimize the number of people exposed and will provide time for people to evacuate. Also, since HVAC systems are usually designed so that air from one zone is recirculated to the same zone rather than to somewhere else, as long as there are no large flows into or out of an area, the HVAC system will not tend to spread agent to other zones. (A system in which each zone manages its own air, without flows that carry air to other zones, is said to be "pressure balanced.") Standard "HVAC Testing and Balancing" procedures will often not yield a pressure-balanced system, as will be discussed in the section on airflow isolation.

Conversely, rapid air flows between zones will expose more people, will allow less time for evacuation, and will carry agent between HVAC zones and thus lead to additional spreading of the agent by the HVAC system. This situation was observed at several locations in several airports.

Because of the potential for rapid and substantial spreading of an agent, the assessment team must look for such large airflows and seek to reduce them. As a starting point, the assessment team should accompany airport HVAC engineers to walk through each building and terminal area, and note whether there are easily perceptible airflows (e.g. drafts that can be felt on the faces of the assessors) between areas (e.g. between the main terminal and the boarding areas). They should note the direction of these airflows, as flows from insecure areas (outside security) into secure areas (inside security) are less desirable than those that flow the other way. Note that pressure balance will tend to shift with weather and drift with time, so seasonal re-checking will be necessary, and more frequent checking is desirable. If a deeper understanding of the airflows is required, the assessment team should proceed with the "moderate" and "hard" assessment methods described in *Appendix B*.

3.2.2   Air supply to critical emergency response functions

If an attack occurs, emergency personnel need to be able to coordinate the response: contact fire/police/hazardous materials teams, coordinate communications, etc. To do these things, security and communications centers need to remain operational, especially in the first few minutes when response is initiated and outside responders are contacted. This will not be possible if a chemical agent is rapidly carried into these critical areas.

If the offices of emergency personnel are adjacent to or share HVAC systems with public areas, then those critical emergency response functions are vulnerable to direct or collateral attack. Agent released in an attack on a public area can spread to the emergency response offices via two primary paths: (1) directly due to airflows as described in the preceding subsection, or (2) by recirculation through the HVAC system.

The assessment team must look for airflows from public spaces to emergency response offices and seek to reduce them. As a starting point, the assessment team should ask airport HVAC engineers to check for perceptible flows from publicly accessible areas to critical areas, and check HVAC design blueprints to see if air handling units mix return air from public areas into supply air for critical areas. If a deeper understanding is required, the assessment team should proceed with the "moderate" and "hard" assessment methods described in *Appendix B*.

3.2.3   HVAC filters, dampers, and fan operations

A component of ensuring proper airflows is ensuring proper filtration and proper operation of HVAC dampers and fans. Filtration, which removes particulates from the air in a building, would typically also remove biological agents. Proper filtration can reduce contamination of the building, exposure of people, or both. In some cases, chemical filtration such as carbon filters may also be present and would remove some chemical agents. The assessment team should work with mechanical maintenance personnel to examine HVAC filters looking for missing filters, proper installation, efficiency and condition, including leaks and bypass.

Proper HVAC damper and fan operation is important for HVAC response to an attack. Dampers must close properly and fans must function as required. The assessment team should work with mechanical maintenance personnel to assess the condition of HVAC damper and fan operations.

3.3 Assessment of Response Capabilities

Airports have numerous resources that may be brought to bear in response to a chem-bio attack. The purpose of the assessment is to help the airport identify these response capabilities, identify important cost-effective upgrades and additions to those capabilities, and to provide a starting point for creating comprehensive response plans.

The assessment must consider all of the following capabilities:
- training of airport employees to recognize overt chem-bio events
- systems and procedures to detect covert bio events

- video capabilities that could provide rapid video access to affected areas
- remote emergency airflow control options
- proper HVAC damper and fan operation
- procedures to manipulate airflow control
- procedures to shelter in place
- procedures to evacuate people
- procedures to decontaminate exposed people
- procedures to detain people at the airport
- procedures to identify exposed people

These are the capabilities that are required to be in place for rapid response. They are discussed further in *Section 6.1, Response Preparation.* These components make up the response procedures, discussed in *Section 6.2.*

3.4 Assessment to Facility Hardening

Once the facility assessment is complete, the next step is facility hardening – upgrading the systems so that they better deter and/or mitigate the consequences of an attack. The recommendations are summarized in a table in *Appendix C: Facility Hardening.* The next section, *Section 4*, discusses hardening of HVAC system physical security systems in order to increase physical deterrents to chem-bio attack. *Section 5* discusses airflow control for passive protection – protection measures that will mitigate the consequences of an attack, even without knowledge of the attack. *Section 6* describes response preparation – the creation of systems and plans for response to an overt attack, in order that the optimal response can be implemented rapidly.

Intentionally left blank.

4. Attack Prevention: Ventilation (HVAC) System Physical Security

<This section removed for this Unlimited Release version.>

Intentionally left blank.

5. Attack Mitigation: Passive Protection through Airflow Control

<This section removed for this Unlimited Release version.>

Intentionally left blank.

6. Attack Mitigation: Active Response

The final section of the guidance involves response – how to prepare to respond to an event and what actions to take in the event that an attack (or sophisticated hoax) is discovered. The possibility of discovery depends on the type of attack and agent. An attack with a fast-acting chemical that produces immediate symptoms will likely be discovered, particularly if airport employees have been adequately trained. An attack with a slower-acting chemical that produces no immediate symptoms, or an attack with a biological agent may not be discovered at all until hours or days after the event. In the unlikely event that there is indication of such an attack, there is likely to be much uncertainty. The response measures suggested in this section reflect the certainty about the event – in less certain events, the response is smaller, perhaps only clearing and cordoning off a very small area; in more certain events, the response may merit evacuating and shutting down the entire airport, at least temporarily.

As stated in the *Introduction* and in the previous two sections, planners should recognize that attack prevention, attack mitigation, and preparation for active response will require substantial planning and thought to identify what actions are or are not worthwhile. In addition to the complexity of determining the cost-benefit of the various improvements, each improvement carries its own set of complexities. This section of the document explains what actions will make an airport safer by providing active protection through active response, but the document does not discuss implementation. To implement these recommendations, it is especially important to resolve issues of communication, decision-making, and prioritization, since confusion in these areas can waste time, possibly with fatal consequences. Many of these issues revolve around the allocation of decision-making responsibility. Here is a small sampling of some of the key questions: Who should be able to initiate evacuation? Who decides whether it is necessary to evacuate to the aircraft operations area? Who decides whether to shut down the airport in response to a possible biological release, with no symptoms yet apparent? Who decides where people will be detained or quarantined, who decides whether such actions are necessary, and how are they implemented? Who communicates with HVAC operators in order to request system shut-down, purge, or other manipulation? Many, many questions such as these must be answered, and people trained accordingly, if pre-event planning is to be useful. Establishing procedures on paper is not enough – practice drills are essential. The implementation of the response procedures requires detailed advanced planning by each airport on an individual basis.

This section of the document discusses the plans and procedures that an airport must establish for its individual circumstances in order to provide rapid response for mitigation of a known or suspected chemo-bio event. *Section 6.1* describes all the pieces that must be in place for that rapid response to occur. *Section 6.2* describes the actual prioritized time-ordered sequence of events that the airport should take in response to a chem-bio event.

6.1 Response Preparation

Plans must be developed, maintained and practiced in order that every airport employee and first responder knows and can implement his/her role in the response. These include plans for communications, crisis management, HVAC control or shutdown, and plans for using response equipment, directing emergency evacuations, and decontaminating people. In addition, well in advance of any event, suitable internal shelter-in-place areas and external congregation areas must be identified. Decisions must be made about whether to purchase personal protection equipment (PPE), what type should be acquired for whom, where it should be stored, and how and when it should be used in an event.

The priority advance preparation tasks are discussed in *Table 6.1* and the subsections below. As in the previous two sections, the tasks are ordered by three levels of protection: Priority I (highest priority), Priority II (high priority), and Priority III (additional important measures). The three levels of priority are meant to indicate the relative level of benefit among the possible measures, to aid airport emergency planners in determining resource allocation (e.g., based on the costs versus benefits of each measure in that particular facility, since cost depends on the current status of that component of the facility).

The first four subsections discuss the Priority I (highest priority) aspects of response preparation: train airport employees to recognize overt chem-bio events (*Subsection 6.1.1*); establish procedures to shelter in place (*Subsection 6.1.2*); establish evacuation procedures (*Subsection 6.1.3*); and establish decontamination procedures (*Subsection 6.1.4*). The next five Subsections discuss Priority II (high priority) measures: establish capability and procedures for remote emergency airflow control options (*Subsection 6.1.5*); establish procedures to detain people at the airport (*Subsection 6.1.6*); establish procedures to locate unknowingly exposed people (*Subsection 6.1.7*); consider pre-screening of vehicles entering the pickup and drop-off areas (*Subsection 6.1.8*); and consider heightened security at curbside and at check-in (*Subsection 6.1.9*). The final two subsections discuss the Priority III (additional important) measures: establish systems and procedures to detect covert bio events (*Subsection 6.1.10*); and modify video capabilities in order to provide rapid video access to affected areas (*Subsection 6.1.11*).

Table 6.1 Attack Mitigation: Response Preparation
Establish and practice procedures to...

Priority I	Priority II	Priority III
• Recognize overt chem-bio events • Shelter in place • Evacuate people • Decontaminate people	• Control airflow remotely • Detain people at airport • Locate unknowingly exposed people • Heighten curbside security	• Detect covert bio events • Obtain video access to affected areas

...in order to maximize the number of survivors.

6.1.1 Train airport employees to recognize overt chem-bio events (Priority I)

Airport employees already have extensive training in recognition of suspicious devices and behaviors. This training should be extended to help them immediately identify possible chem-bio events as well, both by recognizing suspicious devices and behaviors, and also by recognizing early chem-bio symptoms. The key to minimizing the consequences of a chem-bio attack is early recognition and response: the more quickly an attack is recognized, the more quickly people can be evacuated and airflow manipulated to contain (or exhaust, as appropriate) the agent. One of the strengths of airport defense is the number of airport and airline employees present throughout the facility. The employees can be trained to recognize potential chem-bio events and to alert the communications center to begin the response procedures that will be described in *Section 6.2*. In order for training to remain up-to-date, it must be repeated at some reasonable frequency, both to refresh people's minds, and to train new hires. Because the turnover rate of airport employees may be a source of intelligence for attackers, pre-hire security processes are important considerations.

6.1.2 Establish procedures to shelter in place (Priority I)

For some types of events (for example, outdoor chem – or bio if it's known – upwind of the facility) the best response is to shelter in place. The shelter-in-place response requires advance identification of shelter-in-place locations, manipulation of airflow controls in response to the event, and movement of people to the shelter-in-place locations. Procedures must be in place and practiced in order to rapidly shelter in place in response to an event.

6.1.3 Establish procedures to evacuate people (Priority I)

For indoor releases, and for outdoor releases after the concentration inside the facility is greater than outside the facility, evacuation of people from the contaminated facility into fresh air outside will be important for reducing their overall exposure. In the case of a fast-acting chemical agent, people may self-evacuate before emergency response personnel can act. But in other cases, advance planning can facilitate rapid evacuation. Advance planning must include determination of safe evacuation routes and holding areas. Safe holding areas must be upwind of the contamination. They must be large, unenclosed outdoor spaces. Enclosed areas such as courtyards or areas between boarding wings are not safe holding areas; these may retain the agent long after it has dissipated elsewhere. After evacuation, additional procedures might be necessary, such as retention of people for public health or law enforcement reasons, decontamination, and possibly maintaining the security of the airfield operating area. Procedures must be in place and practiced in order to rapidly evacuate people and implement these additional procedures.

6.1.4 Establish procedures to decontaminate exposed people (Priority I)

People who have been exposed to a chemical or biological agent may have residue from that exposure on their skin, hair, clothing, and personal effects. Removal of the agent from these exposed people through the process of decontamination serves two purposes: (1) decontamination stops the on-going additional exposure of those people to that residue, and (2) decontamination prevents people from tracking the agent elsewhere beyond the contaminated part of the airport (such as their cars, homes, medical facilities) and potentially exposing others. Primary decontamination can be accomplished by removal of clothing and scrubbing down with soap and water. Decontamination foam, such as the foam invented at Sandia National Laboratories[21,22] can be used to neutralize the agent before people have access to soap and water and also to decontaminate essential personal items such as identification cards. Plans must be in place in order to rapidly deploy mass decontamination. Speed of deployment is essential both for the health of the exposed people, and also to entice people to remain at the airport for decontamination, which helps contain the tracking of agent. Procedures must be in place to keep track of personal items, and to contain contaminated clothing and decontamination liquids if possible.

6.1.5 Establish capability and procedures for remote emergency airflow control options (Priority II)

Section 6.2 discusses response to a chem-bio release if one is known (or believed) to have occurred. One important component of an emergency response plan is airflow control, particularly shut down of HVAC and exhaust fans. The ability to shut down the HVAC systems and exhaust fans remotely and rapidly must be implemented, preferably in more than one location, in case the primary control center is affected by the event. Single-switch controls should be put in place that enable shutdown of HVAC and exhaust fans for primary HVAC response, as well as any additional airflow control measures such as fire doors, drop-down curtains, or shelter-in-place measures. Airports often have many exhaust fans (bathroom, kitchen, elevators, etc.) that are independent of the HVAC system. Since full airflow control requires that these fans can be turned on or off as part of the emergency response, the airport should consider modifying fan controls if necessary so that these fans can be operated remotely from the same location as the HVAC system.

In addition, single-switch controls could be implemented to perform secondary HVAC responses such as purge, smoke control, or recirculation, to facilitate HVAC manipulation for agent exhaust or containment after the initial response and evacuation. The primary location for these controls should be a place that has continual operator presence, so that they can be manipulated immediately in response to an event. In addition to planning for remote control, advance preparation requires assurance and periodic testing that dampers and fans be in good working order, as established in the section on airflow hardening, and that rapid response capabilities be designed within the capabilities of the system.[*]

In addition to establishing the capability for remote airflow control, airport planners must create protocols for when and how to provide this component response. The HVAC operator must have a clearly established set of procedures to follow for each type of event in each possible release location. The general guidance is recommended in *Section 6.2* on response procedures, but the particulars must be worked out for each location: boarding piers, terminal buildings, HVAC ducts, outdoors, etc. The procedures should be

---

[*] For active response, the faster the damper response, the better (within reason); however, because very rapid damper closing can cause a substantial pressure shock to the duct system and lead to joint separation and leaks, this system must be designed carefully, perhaps including an emergency diversion system for the additional pressure.

documented in a manual available at several independent (but secure) places within the airport and on-line.

6.1.6 Establish procedures to detain people at the airport (Priority II)

In some cases, it may be necessary to detain people at the airport. For example, if there is strong reason to believe they may have been exposed to a contagious biological agent, then for public health reasons, they must be detained at the airport in order to contain the exposure. In another example, if the exposed people must be decontaminated, then they must be detained at the airport until they have been decontaminated. In yet another example, if there is reason to believe that the perpetrator of the attack may still be at the airport, then for law enforcement reasons, it may be necessary to detain people until that person is identified. There are many reasons why people should be detained at the airport, and there must be procedures in place to implement this. These procedures may involve blocking roadways; closing parking exits; stopping circulation of busses onto, off of, and within the airport; shutting down or restricting access to any rapid transit; and closing the airport entrance and exits(s). These procedures may involve bringing in additional police for crowd control. They certainly must involve provision of adequate shelter, food, water, restrooms, and medical care for the detainees. Plans and procedures for all of these cases must be well planned in advance. Quarantine laws differ in each state, and part of emergency planning must be determining who has the authority to impose a quarantine and how that decision will be made.

6.1.7 Establish procedures to locate unknowingly exposed people (Priority II)

A bio attack is unlikely to be discovered for days, or at least hours, so procedures to identify potentially exposed people are important to facilitate rapid treatment. This is complicated by the fact that by the time an attack is discovered, many of the victims will be long gone from the airport, perhaps to distant destinations, and that airlines as a rule do not share passenger information. Press coverage of the event can lead some people to self-identify, but many people may need to be traced. Establishing tracking procedures with the airlines, as well as other companies that have an airport business, such as limousine, taxi, and rental car companies, or merchants in the airport, will facilitate identification of victims in the event of an attack.

6.1.8 Consider pre-screening of vehicles entering the pickup and drop-off areas (Priority II)

For an terrorist attack outside an airport building, the easiest way to bring a device to the airport is in a car, truck, or van. Trucks and vans are particularly attractive to a terrorist because they provide a large work and storage space that is invisible from the outside. Vehicle delivery is attractive for both a conventional bomb and for a chem-bio release device. To reduce this possibility, cars attempting to approach terminal pick-up and drop-off areas can be stopped and checked before nearing the building. Several levels of security are possible: (1) minimal: watch incoming traffic and stop vehicles that seem suspicious; (2) moderate: stop all trucks and vans for inspection, and inspect the trunk of any passenger cars that seem suspicious; (3) high: look into every vehicle, including luggage space, and hand-check any luggage that looks suspicious. In any of these cases, security officers should be alert for both conventional explosives and for chem-bio devices, which might be recognized from modifications to the vehicle or to luggage; presence of hoses, nozzles, or other signs of liquid- or gas-handling; and tanks that could contain chemical or biological agent. Tanks containing agent might appear to be innocent, such as propane tanks for gas-powered camping stoves or barbecues. Even a small tank could contain enough agent for a highly lethal attack. A terrorist device might be designed to look like welding equipment, a pesticide sprayer, or some other apparatus designed for use with tanks and hoses.

6.1.9   Consider heightened security at curbside and at check-in (Priority II)

The security screening for passengers is a significant deterrent to a terrorist attempting to bring a weapon or terror device into an airport. However, a release in the check-in area or in the line waiting to pass through security would not require bringing a device through the security checkpoint and might even allow the terrorist to escape after triggering the release. To reduce this possibility, security personnel can watch people arriving at the airport for (1) unusual luggage or luggage that appears to have been modified; (2) someone assembling or preparing a device to be triggered, perhaps under the guise of re-packing of luggage; (3) someone abandoning luggage and exiting the building. Any of these should trigger a challenge by security personnel.

6.1.10   Establish systems and procedures to detect covert bio events (Priority III)

Implement systems to track employee absenteeism and health. Personnel databases may already contain such information for a subset of people regularly at the airport. An out-of-the-ordinary pattern of illness could be used to identify a bio agent attack more quickly than Public Health could track hospital admissions back to the airport.

Perform regular (e.g. daily) testing of ventilation filters for biological agents of concern. Such testing, which costs several hundred dollars per test, can determine that a biological release has occurred. Less frequent testing would still identify a release, but whether the test result would identify the attack before epidemiologic tracking or not would depend on the relative timing and speed of the two approaches.

6.1.11   Modify video capabilities in order to provide rapid video access to affected areas (Priority III)

Many airports have extensive closed circuit television surveillance systems already in place for security purposes. In the event of a detected attack, these could be utilized to provide visual information to decision-makers in the communications center or the emergency operations center. Systems could be set up that would select the appropriate cameras for display in order to provide immediate CCTV surveillance of affected areas. Particularly in the event of a fast-acting chemical agent, decision-makers could rapidly assess the extent of the attack by viewing the physical symptoms of the people in the area, and use this information in planning evacuation and additional response.

6.2 Response Procedures

For severe chem-bio incidents, response within a few minutes is critical to containing agent spread and saving lives. If twenty minutes pass before responses are taken, the effectiveness of response measures may be significantly reduced. Plans, tools, and training must be in place to support rapid decision-making and implementation. For releases of highly toxic chemicals such as sarin or biological agents such as anthrax spores, response in the first few minutes can greatly reduce contamination and casualties. The advance planning and preparation required for rapid response was discussed in *Section 6.1 Response Preparation*. This section discusses when to use which of these pre-established procedures.

The appropriate response procedures depend primarily on whether the attack occurs indoors or outdoors, and to a lesser extent whether the attack agent is chemical or biological. The simple guideline is the following: if the event trigger is observed outdoors, then the attack is likely outdoors; if the event trigger is observed indoors and not outdoors, then the attack is likely indoors. If the event trigger is an attack on the HVAC system (including its outdoor fresh air intakes), then respond as if the attack is indoors.

A previously released LBNL document[11] suggests the following approach to distinguishing between a chemical and biological attack:

> If you know a release of some kind has occurred, determine whether it is a chemical release by looking for symptoms. A biological agent rarely causes immediate symptoms; a chemical agent almost always does.
>
> Symptoms of exposure to toxic chemicals, including chemical warfare agents, include one or more of:
> - pinpoint pupils, leading to a perception of darkness;
> - dilated pupils (caused by come chemicals, but not chemical warfare agents);
> - dizziness;
> - runny nose;
> - clammy skin or perspiration;
> - difficulty breathing;
> - nausea and/or vomiting;
> - blurred vision or blindness;
> - seizures;
> - loss of bladder control;
> - loss of consciousness, or death.
>
> If people in the building exhibit sudden onset of some of these symptoms, a chemical release may be responsible. Food poisoning could have some of the same symptoms but would usually not strike many people nearly simultaneously.

The same document[11] also discusses distinguishing between an indoor and outdoor release:

> Since a biological release will generally not cause immediate symptoms, knowledge of the location, and even occurrence, of a biological release will usually depend on either direct observation of the release event..., or a warning from a law enforcement agency or other source. Lacking such evidence, detecting the source for a biological release may not be possible.
>
> However, whether the source of a chemical release is indoors or outdoors can usually be determined.... Except for a release near a building's air intake [or open door in a

negatively-pressurized building], it would take a very large or very toxic outdoor release to cause immediate severe symptoms indoors. Such releases are not impossible, especially for industrial accidents (e.g., Bhopal, India in December 1984). If there is uncertainty as to where the release occurred or is occurring, look outside – if people are getting very ill inside from an outdoor source, then there will normally be visible evidence outdoors: dead or dying birds and wildlife, people collapsing on the sidewalks, [airfield operating area], etc. If these signs aren't present, the source is probably indoors, or in (or near) one of the building's air intakes.

Some chemical agents have delayed effects, so the severity of a chemical attack might not be apparent immediately. If symptoms of a chemical attack are noted, do not discount the possibility of an attack just because exposed people do not display critical medical problems right away.

The next two subsections describe response guidelines: *Response Guidelines for Indoor Release* in *Subsection 6.2.1*; and *Response Guidelines for Outdoor Release* in *Subsection 0*.

6.2.1   *Response Guidelines for Indoor Release*
<This section removed for this Unlimited Release version.>

6.2.2   *Response Procedures for Outdoor Release*
<This section removed for this Unlimited Release version.>

7. Summary and Conclusions

<This section removed for this Unlimited Release version.>

Intentionally left blank.

Appendix A. Report Card for Airport Chem-Bio Protection and Response

<This section removed for this Unlimited Release version.>

Intentionally left blank.

Appendix B. Assessment of Airflow Characteristics

<This section removed for this Unlimited Release version.>

Intentionally left blank.

Appendix C. Facility Hardening

<This section removed for this Unlimited Release version.>

Intentionally left blank.

Appendix D. Response Guidelines Cards

<This section removed for this Unlimited Release version.>

REFERENCES

1. U.S. Department of Energy. Chemical & Biological National Security Program FY02 Annual Report. Washington, D.C.: U.S. Government Printing Office, 2002.

2. Donna Edwards, Susanna Gordon, et al. *Tracer Release Experiments at San Francisco International Airport To Improve Preparedness against Chemical and Biological Terrorism*, SAND2001-8380 (OUO), Sandia National Laboratories, Livermore, CA, June 2001.

3. Susanna Gordon, Donna Edwards, et al. *Assessments of San Francisco International Airport to Improve Preparedness Against Chemical and Biological Terrorism*, SAND2003-8554 (OUO), Sandia National Laboratories, Livermore, CA, September 2003.

4. Richard Griffith, et al. *Biological Defense Initiative Albuquerque Testbed: Access Control Point Monitoring (Albuquerque Airport)*, SAND2003-2070 (OUO), Sandia National Laboratories, Albuquerque, NM, June 2003.

5. The National Institute of Occupational Safety and Health. *Guidance for Protecting Building Environments from Airborne Chemical, Biological, or Radiological Attacks*, 2002. http://www.cdc.gov/niosh/bldvent/2002-139.html.

6. William. A. Swansiger and Anne D. Platt, et al. *Guide to Defending DOE Sites Against Chemical Attacks: Volume I – SNM Sites,* SAND2003-8602 (UCNI), Sandia National Laboratories, October 2003.

7. William. A. Swansiger and Anne D. Platt, et al. *Guide to Defending DOE Sites Against Chemical Attacks: Volume II –Office Buildings,* SAND2003-8603 (OUO), Sandia National Laboratories, October 2003.

8. Ronald Dykhuizen et al. *Protection of the Philadelphia Mint Facility from Chemical, Biological, and Radiological Threats*, SAND2003-2645 (OUO), Sandia National Laboratories, Albuquerque, NM, July 2003.

9. Ronald Dykhuizen and Richard Griffith. *Protecting U.S. Mint Facilities from Chem/Bio/Rad Threats*, SAND2003-4781 (OUO), Sandia National Laboratories, Albuquerque, NM, January 2004.

10. Ronald Dykhuizen et al. *Protection of the San Francisco Mint Facility from Chemical, Biological, and Radiological Threats*, SAND2003-4782 (OUO), Sandia National Laboratories, Albuquerque, NM, January 2004.

11. Phillip N. Price, et al. *Protecting Buildings from a Biological or Chemical Attack: Actions to Take Before or During a Release*, LBNL/PUB-51959, Lawrence Berkeley National Laboratory, Berkeley, January 2003.

12. U.S. Army Edgewood Chemical Biological Center and the U.S. Army Corps of Engineers Protective Design Center. *Protecting Buildings and their Occupants from Airborne Hazards*, TI 853-01, October 2001.

13. A. Boyd and J. P. Sullivan. Emergency Preparedness for Transit Terrorism, TCRP Synthesis 27. Washington, D.C.: National Academy Press, 1997.

14. D. E. Kaplan. "Aum Shinrikyo (1995)." Toxic Terror: Assessing Terrorist Use of Chemical and Biological Weapons. Ed. J. B. Tucker. Cambridge: MIT Press, 2000.

15. W.S. Carus. "The Rajneeshees (1984)." Toxic Terror: Assessing Terrorist Use of Chemical and Biological Weapons. Ed. J. B. Tucker. Cambridge: MIT Press, 2000.

16. L.A. Barakat et al. "Fatal Inhalational Anthrax in a 94-Year-Old Connecticut Woman." Journal of the American Medical Association 287 (2002): 863-8.

17. B. Mina et al. "Fatal Inhalational Anthrax with Unknown Source of Exposure in a 61-Year-Old Woman in New York City." Journal of the American Medical Association 287 (2002): 858-62.

18. "Hole in Rome Tunnel Linked to US Embassy Plot." The Guardian 25 February 2002.

19. "'Terror Tunnels' Found in Rome." BBC News 24 February 2002, 15:31 GMT.

20. Jane's Chem-Bio Handbook, www.janes.com.

21. M. Tucker and C. Williams, *SNL decon formulation for mitigation and decontamination of CBW agents*, SAND2000-0619, Sandia National Laboratories, February 2000.

22. M. Tucker and C. Williams, *SNL decon formulation for mitigation and decontamination of chemical and biological warfare agents : overview*, SAND2000-0625, Sandia National Laboratories, February 2000.

Intentionally left blank.

FURTHER READING

The National Institute of Occupational Safety and Health's *Guidance for Protecting Building Environments from Airborne Chemical, Biological, or Radiological Attacks* (2002) provides general guidance for defense of buildings against airborne threats. http://www.cdc.gov/niosh/bldvent/2002-139.html

The U.S. Army Corps of Engineers' *Protecting Buildings and their Occupants from Airborne Hazards*" TI 853-01 (2001) provides similar general guidance with a somewhat different scope than the NIOSH document above.

A "pocket-sized guide for first responders" which contains a comprehensive but concise review of chemical and biological agents, effects, and treatments is presented in the *Jane's Chem-Bio Handbook* by Sidell, Patrick, and Dashiell and published by Jane's Information Group. http://www.janes.com/company/catalog/chem_bio_hand.shtml

Information regarding protection of facilities in particular against terrorism and violent crime is provided by another Jane's publication, *Jane's Facility Security Handbook*. http://www.janes.com/company/catalog/facility_security.shtml

The Centers for Disease Control and Prevention's website contains information on biological, chemical, and radiological agents as well as treatments and response options. Also includes guidelines on handling suspicious letters and packages. http://www.bt.cdc.gov

The Johns Hopkins Center for Civilian Biodefense posts information on all aspects of bioterrorism preparedness and response, from medical diagnosis and treatment to political issues to upcoming conferences. http://www.hopkins-biodefense.org

The Monterey Institute of International Studies maintains a resource page with information on chemical and biological agents, overviews on the capabilities of various states to produce weapons of mass destruction, and a chronology of incidents in which such weapons have been used. http://cns.miis.edu/research/cbw

The U.S. Army Medical Research Institute of Infectious Diseases (USAMRIID) provides reference material on biological weapons, including the latest edition of *Medical Management Of Biological Casualties Handbook* and links to other relevant websites. http://www.usamriid.army.mil/education/instruct.html

The U.S. Army Medical Research Institute of Chemical Defense (USAMRICD) provides reference material on chemical weapons, including the latest edition of *Medical Management of Chemical Casualties Handbook* and links to other relevant websites. http://ccc.apgea.army.mil/reference_materials/obtainmaterials.asp

Though somewhat dated, *Chemical and Biological Terrorism: Research and Development to Improve Civilian Medical Response* by the Institute of Medicine (National Academy Press, 1999) provides excellent overviews of personal protective equipment, patient decontamination, mass triage, detection of chemical and biological agents, and therapeutics. http://www.nap.edu/catalog/6364.html

Bioterrorism and Biocrimes: the Illicit Use of Biological Agents in the 20th Century by W. Seth Carus of the National Defense University (Washington, D.C.) is a frequently updated compilation of all known incidents involving biological agents since 1900. http://www.ndu.edu/centercounter/prolif_publications.htm

Toxic Terror: Assessing Terrorist Use of Chemical and Biological Weapons edited by Jonathan B. Tucker (MIT, 2000) contains in-depth examinations of twelve prominent groups or individuals who allegedly acquired or employed chemical or biological agents. The case studies include the Aum Shinrikyo cult, which released sarin nerve gas in the Tokyo subway in 1995.

Biohazard: The Chilling True Story of the Largest Covert Biological Weapons Program in the World–Told from Inside by the Man Who Ran It by Ken Alibek with Stephen Handelman (Delta, 2000) describes the Soviet Union's formidable research program to develop weapons from agents such as smallpox.

Germs: Biological Weapons and America's Secret War by Judith Miller, Stephen Engelberg, William J. Broad (Simon & Schuster, 2001) is written by three reporters from the *New York Times* and provides a readable introduction to biological weapons and bioterrorism.

UNCLASSIFIED UNLIMITED RELEASE

Initial Distribution

10	MS 9201	Donna Edwards, 8112
1	MS 9201	Susanna Gordon, 8112
1	MS 0899	Technical Library, 9616
3	MS 9018	Central Technical Files, 8945-1
1	MS 9021	Classification Office, 8511 for Technical Library, MS 0899, 9616
1	MS 9021	Classification Office, 8511 For DOE/OSTI

Lawrence Berkeley National Laboratory
One Cyclotron Road
Berkeley, CA 94720
Attn: Ashok Gadgil, MS 90-3058 (5 copies)
Phillip Price, MS 90-3058